PASSIVE I
STRATEGIES:

How to Manifest Wealth, Make Money and Live a Prosperous and Successful Life

Carmelo Parisi

considered an endorsement from the trademark holder.

TABLE OF CONTENTS

INTRODUCTION

Passive Income does not require constant time and effort to produce money. Passive Income is an intelligent way to earn money closely related to the concept of financial freedom.

My mission with this book is to give you the critical information to help your business produce as much passive income as possible. If I achieve this, my mission will be accomplished.

Passive Income is money that you continue to earn without it requiring your time or effort.

In other words, something that you created, rented or invested in and that, after some time, generates profits month after month without investing any more money or time.

But it must be said that passive Income is NOT easy to obtain; it requires time and effort. Therefore, you have to be committed to creating many sources of Passive Income.

For example, imagine your favorite singer. Well... from that song he created more than 20 years ago, he is still earning money without even having to sing it again. Thanks in this case to copyright.

The same goes for a writer and a book. Paulo Coelho continues to make a lot of money with The Alchemist without adding a single line of text.

The landlord of a flat. He bought a flat and now rents it out, which brings him a profit every month. In this case, he needed capital to get started, but it serves as an example.

Passive Income is all income that is earned even if you stop working. An employee who is dependent on a salary must work continuously to continue receiving his salary. When he leaves his job, he stops earning Income immediately. However, passive income continues to be generated after you stop working for it. This is a great advantage because once earned; the individual can create Income in other ways and continue to receive the previous Income.

After writing a book, you can collect passive Income in the form of royalties for years and, in the meantime, open a car-cleaning franchise. An employee cannot leave their job to go to another job and expect to continue receiving the first job.

Of course, I have written prominent examples for you, but there are thousands of passive income ideas.

Passive Income is a different way of saying "earning money without working."

But there is something important I should point out before you confuse the concept.

Generating passive income is not about waiting for money to fall from the sky. The idea is to structure an income stream to flow into our bank accounts or wallets without us doing anything for it.

But in principle, passive Income requires a lot of work.

People who create passive Income find themselves working hard for days, weeks, months, and even years to get everything set up and running automatically.

Now, passive Income is not necessarily something that is generated in a steady stream.

That is, if you make $100 this month, $80 the next month, and $104 the next month, that's fine, as long as it doesn't require your time.

And before you ask me, what are the benefits of passive income?

Well. I like to use the same example every time.

Imagine you have a salary of €1,000. And tomorrow, you get fired. What will happen? You'll earn €0. You will have a BIG problem.

Now imagine you have ten mini-salaries of €100. They add up to €1,000 in total. And tomorrow, you lose 2 of those ten sources of Income. What will happen? You will still be earning €800. You will still have NO problems in your life.

Therefore, passive Income offers the following benefits:

- Diversify Income without depending on one in particular.

- Security that tomorrow you will not run out of Income.

- Freedom.

- No income limit.

- No geographical limit. You can generate passive income from anywhere in the world.

- More time for what matters.

Knowing the above, you are now ready to discover how to generate that desired passive Income today.

How to generate passive Income without investing?

Now, this sounds great, but it sounds like an arduous and challenging process.

And indeed, to some extent, it is.

But I don't think it's any more difficult than working for an active income in a little more time.

Let me explain: If you are an employee, you will usually have to spend 8 hours a day for five days a week structuring someone else's Income with your work... whatever it is.

I reckon, to create a passive income, you wouldn't need more than 2 to 4 hours a day...

Of course, you have to choose something that you like, and that is profitable...

But the most important thing is that creating and structuring a passive income is much less work than enriching someone else with a job.

And if you have a job right now, you can start creating wealth in your spare time.

All it takes is commitment.

I'm sure it's not the first time you've asked yourself this question, but have you found a solution?

I can imagine you from 9 am to 7 pm behind the computer screen at your workplace (if you are lucky enough to have a job).

A job that does NOT motivate you, and you are just waiting for the weekend to come and find a reason to smile.

Good. I have good news and bad news. Which one should we start with?

Well, since you can't answer me, we'll choose the bad one.

The bad news is that it will take a lot of time and effort. That's what happens when you want to get started without investing anything.

The good news is that there are ways to generate passive Income WITHOUT investing anything.

We've all had a beginning, and all beginnings are with little money. I can assure you.

There are countless examples; here are a few:

- **Dividends:** Companies, at least the well-managed ones, generate profits consistently. A part of these profits are reinvested in their own business to keep growing, and another part is given to you, for your pretty face, because you are an owner/shareholder (this is dividends).

Most big companies, such as Pepsi, Adidas, Apple... are listed on the stock exchange, and their shares can be bought from home after opening an account with any broker. Smaller companies, such as your friend's fruit shop, are not listed. However, the system is the same: if you convince him to buy a share of the business, you will receive dividends from the company just like him or any other owner.

- **Caution:** You have to distinguish between "being a shareholder or owner of a company" and "working in the company." If you own a hardware store and work in it every day from 9 to 5, you have a job, even if the business's legal form is a partnership.

If you have employees who run the business and meet with the manager once a quarter to see how things are going, you are the owner and have passive income.

- **Royalties:** The author of a book, a song, a photograph, etc., can be paid automatically every time a copy of their work is sold in physical or virtual shops.

- **Rents:** The owner of a house or a parking space charges rent every month for ceding the usufruct (a legal word that fits well and means "right to use") of his property to another person.

- **Commissions:** Some physical and online shops offer commissions and affiliate programs to the public. Anyone can sign up and try to get customers for these shops, and they get a commission in the form of a percentage or a fixed payment without having to be directly involved in the transaction, without handling the payment, without sending the book to your readers, or dealing with returns.

A little higher up, you have a button called "Best investment books," which are the ones I recommend to readers. If you buy them, Amazon pays me a commission from its profit (without raising the price to you).

- **Multi-level marketing:** Many multi-level companies offer the possibility to sell products in exchange for a commission and, also, the person who signs up can offer this possibility to other people.

When new people sign up thanks to your recommendation and make sales, you will also receive a commission from the customers of these new salespeople who have joined the system thanks to you. Each multi-level company's terms and conditions vary widely, and some reward activity rather than building a network to generate passive income.

At what point can it be considered utterly Passive Income?

The truth is that some income is more passive than others, requiring more involvement and less.

An example of very passive Income (the ones we are interested in since we are lazy and the less we work, the better) are dividends from consolidated and stable companies. If you had bought IBM shares in 2000, you would have started receiving a cash dividend every quarter from the company.

Today, after 15 years and without you having had to move from the sofa, you would still be receiving your quarterly cash on time. Moreover, in this case, the dividend has been growing little by little, and today it is ten times higher.

Not bad, eh? Hands up whoever is earning ten times more than in the year 2000 thanks to hard work in a conventional job.

The same goes for bank deposits. If you have a deposit in the bank, you will receive regular interest until you die, and then your heirs will continue to receive it without you having to do anything at all. Of course, the interest on a deposit is tiny, so I prefer dividends, which also tend to grow over time. Like everything else in life, they have their drawbacks, and you will discover them here in this book.

You don't have to do ANY work at all when you have shares in companies or bank deposits?

Correct, it is unnecessary, but that does not mean that you should not move around and check from time to time if any bank or company offers you more for your money, lest they are paying you less than what you could get elsewhere.

Now let's look at a counterexample, which could be renting a student flat. You have an old flat near the university, you put four even older pieces of furniture in it (I hope your face falls off in shame if you do this for real, how can people think of trying to rent real pigsties) and in the summer you go around the area, and the university was looking for tenants.

The phone starts ringing, and you spend a few weeks showing the flat until you get four students to occupy the four rooms you have. You talk to your friend, who also has a flat to rent, ask him for his contract and copy it down. You go to sign the contract with the tenants. A month later, a tap breaks, and you have to go and change it.

Six weeks later, a student tells you that he is leaving, that he has been accepted at the prestigious University of Harvard, and you have to keep looking for tenants. After a while, you have a default, and it turns out... seriously, this is passive income? It's Chinese torture!

Passive Income Requirements

Now, going back to the initial question, there are specific requirements that a Passive Income must have:

- **A Passive Income Must Be Scalable:** regardless of the amount of money at the beginning, this Income must always be able to grow, up to the limit that we want it to... and not, as far as we are forced to (as in a job).

- **Passive Income Is Payments from Other People:** It's obvious. Where else would the money come from? You have to get other people to give you their money all the time. One way is to have the same people pay you month after month, or new people are coming in, and you have a steady income with a fresh cycle of people paying.

- **Passive Income Is Value Generation:** If you don't generate value, how do you expect those people to pay you? Ideally, your revenue structure should allow you to benefit people to the point where they are interested in paying you for the benefit they receive.

- **Passive Income Is Systems:** A system is a set of elements that transforms an input into an output... like the digestive system (which transforms food into nutrients and other things). A passive income must be a system that transforms a need combined with value generation... into money.

- **Passive Income Should Be as Automatic as Possible: If** your passive Income requires a lot of work after it is up and running, it may not be as passive.

The above are the main characteristics of passive Income.

Another definition of Passive Income

Because of the above, it is not easy to establish what is active, semi-passive, and passive Income. The renter in the previous paragraph did not have to get up in the morning every day to work for the property from 9 to 5, of course, but... the poor guy can't go on holiday in peace. So, where do we classify this Income?

After much thought, I have decided on the following definition. It could have been another more flexible or stricter one, but I think my proposal may be generally accepted. Here it goes:

A passive income is generated from an asset that can be bought, sold and bequeathed, and continues to be generated after not working at all for the asset that produces it for 90 days at a time.

Given this definition, the following statements are valid:

IBM dividends are passive Income because I can go 90 days without paying any attention to the company and, besides, I can sell my shares or leave them an inheritance to my children.

Renting the flat to students is not passive Income. My successors inherited the flat, but I cannot go on holiday for 90 days with my mobile phone switched off.

Renting the flat is passive Income if I talk to the estate agent in my neighborhood, and we agree that they take care of absolutely everything and pay me the rent every month after deducting their services. I will charge less, but in return, my Income will be passive.

Yes! As you have just seen, renting the flat can be a passive income... or it can be not! It all depends on how you set it up. In other words:

Automation, system building, and delegation

These three interrelated concepts have one thing in common: you get out of the way. If you have to be behind to collect rent, it's not passive income if you delegate to the real estate agency, yes.

If you have to promote your book's website personally and when the orders arrive, you have to go to the post office to send the copies; you have no passive income. If you agree with a company and take care of selling your work in their shops while you are in town having a great meal and enjoying the excellent weather, it is passive income.

What about a website?

Once again, it depends. Is the website a blog that talks about you, Juanito Pérez, and your readers come in every day to read your adventures?

Then it's not passive income. Sure, you can automate your posts for the next 90 days and enjoy life (an excellent choice if you do that, by the way), but you fail in point number 1: you can't sell your website.

Being a personal business, when Pepito Fernandez buys your website, nobody will go to read his exploits so that Pepito Fernandez won't buy your website. When you decide to close it down, you won't get any liquidation money out of it.

However, suppose you have a non-personal website that sells sunglasses or publishes cute pictures of kittens and generates Income through advertising. In that case, you do have passive Income because you can sell it and automate it to at least have 90 days of peace of mind.

The definition of passive Income is debatable. Anything that falls between the definition mentioned before and the 9 to 5 working hours can be called semi-passive Income, with varying degrees of passivity.

Most Income can be automated, delegated, or generated through systems. Consequently, the same Income can be active, semi-passive, or passive.

All we need is an internet connection and a device to work from.

It's not a bed of roses, you will have competition, and you will have to dedicate a lot of time and effort, but I can guarantee you one thing, sitting on your couch at home is not going to change your situation, trying to create passive Income will.

So leave any excuse aside and start creating, without fear, without complexes.

Finally, there are two aspects that we have not discussed passive Income: temporality and instability. Everything in life comes to an end, and so does passive Income. Some last for a few months; others can last for more than a century and be passed on from generation to generation. As far as their stability is concerned, some are predictable, stable, and growing, and others are very volatile.

As this introduction is already getting rather long and intends to put this and what is considered passive Income here in context, I will leave these two points to be expanded upon in the book, like all the others we have briefly discussed here. Now, let's generate passive Income!

To help you change your thinking, I know eight truths about money that millionaires embrace

1. Money can solve most problems

Most people have a dysfunctional, adversarial relationship with money. But, if you want to start attracting money, stop seeing it as your enemy and think of it as one of your greatest allies.

The typical truth is that people tend to view money as an enemy. Great people know that money is a critical tool that presents options and opportunities.

They also know that you won't be happy with it if you're not happy without ith it. But while money has little to do with happiness, it's one of the essential tools in our life.

The wealthiest people see money for all the good things that it can provide, such as freedom, opportunity, possibility, and abundance — and are not afraid to admit that, logically, it can solve most problems.

2. Getting rich has little to do with your level of education

Have you ever walked into a wealthy person's home, and one of the first things you see is an extensive library of books that they used to educate themselves on becoming more successful.

Most incredibly wealthy and successful people are college dropouts.

While the rich don't necessarily put much stock in furthering wealth through formal education, they appreciate the power of learning long after high school or college is over and chooses to constantly self-educate.

Building a fortune isn't necessarily about being smarter; it's about knowing what you want and being laser-focused on getting it, no matter how long it might take or how hard you have to work.

It's simple, but not easy. Self-made millionaires know that getting rich has little to do with intelligence and everything to do with focus and persistence.

3. Love what you do

If you do what you love, the money tends to follow; instead of setting out to find work with the most profit potential, focus on jobs that have the most fulfillment potential. Once you find it, invest much time and energy into your work to become one of the most competent people in your field of what you do.

4. You'll be rewarded with uncommon wealth."

If you do what you love, other traits are required to be successful and will become easier.

The masses think about how much they can get paid to do something, while a wealthy person figures out what they love to do and then finds out how to make money doing it. The wealthiest, most successful people pursue their passions.

5. You don't have to have money to make money

A wealthy person knows that money is always available because rich people are always looking for the best investments and superior performers to make those investments profitable.

The wealthiest people focus on coming up with the most innovative ideas first. Then, they aren't afraid to fund their future from other people's pockets.

The middle-class cliché is that you have to have money to make money is limiting at its best and destructive at worst. The truth is you have to have great ideas that solve problems to make money...Creative ideas are scarce, but most people are so focused on where the money is coming from that they ignore their opinions.

6. Money doesn't just fall into your lap — you have to go after it

Wealthy people ask, Why not me? I'm as good as anyone else, and I deserve to be more. If I serve others by solving problems, why shouldn't I be rewarded with a fortune? And, since they believe, their behavior moves them toward the manifestation of their dreams and aspirations.

The millionaires not only actively pursue their ambitious financial goals until they're met, but they expect to make money.

While the middle class tends to keep playing the waiting game, the rich define specific wealth goals and create a concrete plan to achieve them.

"You're not going to be discovered, saved, or made rich by an outside force, "If you want a lot of money, build your ship. No one is coming to your rescue."

7. The quickest way to wealth is self-employment

The masses almost guarantee themselves a life of financial mediocrity by staying in a job with a modest salary and yearly pay raises.

While the world-class continue to start businesses and build fortunes, ordinary people settle for steady paychecks and miss out on the opportunity to accumulate the greatest of wealth.

It's not only that there aren't world-class performers who punch a time clock for a paycheck, but for most, this is the slowest path to prosperity, promoted as the safest. The great ones know that self-employment is the fastest road to wealth.

Ordinary people choose to get paid based on their time on a steady salary or hourly rate — while rich people choose to get paid based on results. What's more, rich people are typically self-employed and determine the size of their paycheck.

You need to stop telling yourself that getting rich is outside of your control. The truth is that making money is for all of us.

8. How do you start thinking like a rich person? Study them.

Anyone can become a millionaire, getting rich beings with the way you think and what you believe about making money ... The secret has always been the same: thinking

The Best Ways to Become a Millionaire

Develop Your Career and Expertise

Most millionaires are millionaires because they worked hard and found a way to earn a lot of money. They earned degrees, professional designations, and certifications to increase their knowledge, and they are often willing to spend time doing low-paid internships and apprenticeships to learn their craft more. As they became experts, they began to earn more.

Create a Financial Plan

Whether you hire a financial adviser or decide to go solo, you need a plan of action. How much will you save? Where will you invest, and when? What if you get laid off from your job, or you have a financial setback? Try to prepare for as many outcomes as possible. You don't always imagine things as the worst-case scenario, but you should know what you'll do if you get off track.

Save Diligently and Invest for Growth

Having an emergency fund available so that you don't have to dip into your savings once more, have a focused plan for how much you'll save every paycheck. If you can put those savings in an account that you will never touch, you'll be well on your way to building that nest egg. A bonus point is if you can put it in an account with a high-interest rate.

The biggest mistake that people make that keeps them from reaching their millionaire status is they upscale their lifestyle when their income rises. When your income goes up, the first thing you should increase is how you contribute to savings.

You can become a millionaire by spending less than you make, saving diligently, and investing appropriately. How much you need to keep depends on how much time you have and the return rate you will earn.

Make Smart Investments

Being a smart investor doesn't always mean playing with the stock market and hoping you'll get in on the ground floor for the next Apple or Amazon. Figure out which investments work for you; this might mean maxing out your 401(k) or opening an IRA, or even just a money market account. The idea is to avoid having all of your savings in inactive tabs. You need to make your money work a little bit.

Neither do you have to use an excessive amount of your income for investment purposes? Find an amount that you're comfortable with, and then you can start there.

Build a Business

The situation is different when you make a product. You have to figure out how to market it, manufacture it, and distribute that product profitably.

If you are in a service business, creating a duplicable business model can be challenging; typically, the place is in your area of expertise, and you are the business. You have to figure out a way to train others to do what you do to work on your business rather than work in your industry.

Create Intellectual Property

If you have an idea or achieve mastery at what you do, think about how you might create subscriptions, licenses, or franchises to expand on your position in your industry.

The same thing is real for surgeons and dentists who design and improve instruments.

Software developers turn their ideas and code into intellectual property.

Artists, such as actors and singers, essentially turn themselves and their "image" into a marketable organization.

Electricians, plumbers, woodworkers, masons, chefs, and other craftspeople may create new tools to use in their industry.

Intellectual property includes things like books, trademarks, patents, songs, scripts, and art. Some professors use their expertise to write books and consult in their field.

Other subject-matter experts design seminars, workshops, and training programs to sell their books and other materials.

Hire a Financial Adviser

Even though you may be taking what you think are all the right steps, you should still consult a professional adviser.

Wealth advisers can help you create a road map for your savings goals, point you to wise investments, and identify areas where you can reduce expenses or get greater returns on those investments.

Invest in Real Estate

Real estate millionaires put in a lot of hard work early on in their life, but it pays off later in the form of residual rental income, not to mention rising real estate values over time.

Those who develop real estate projects also take on significant risks; some pay off big, and others create losses. Be prepared for ups and downs with your real estate ventures

Tips of a millionaire mindset

1. Develop a written financial plan.

The success experienced by those who do this occurs regardless of their relative wealth. Likewise, the failure of those who do not follow a plan is unrelated to their wealth.

In my experience, the most significant difference between those on the right path vs. those on the wrong way is the amount of time and effort they put into conceiving a plan for their finances.

But taking the time to create a plan and see it work through is the one thing that all financially successful people have in common.

I want to stress these two inputs because they are fundamental to all financial planning regardless of how huge either of them is.

In a financial plan, when planning for a more secure future, two inputs are indispensable: how much money you have and how much money you spend.

One of the main reasons why some people can never become a millionaire is that they haven't written a financial plan.

Developing a financial plan forces you to take action instead of just talking. It also guides you in making the right decisions to achieve all of your dreams and goals.

2. When creating a financial plan

- Focus on what matters the most and don't obsess over the past.
- Focus on what you control by listing your general expenses in your budget, and with the income that is left over, list the discretionary categories.
- Focus on your future by anticipating how much your future self is going to need to survive.

3. Associate with millionaires.

The reality is that millionaires think differently from the middle class about money, and there's much to gain by being in their presence.

Exposure to people who are more successful than you are has the potential to expand your thinking and catapult your income.

We'll become like the people we associate ourselves with, which is why winners are attracted to winners.

In most cases, your net worth reflects the level of your closest friends, for Business Insider.

This isn't a new philosophy. It's been around ever since Andrew Carnegie embraced the Master Mind principle.

4. Upgrade your skills and knowledge.

You need to read at least 30 minutes a day, listen to relevant podcasts while driving and seek out mentors vigorously," Tucker Hughes, who wrote, who became a millionaire at just the age of 22.

You don't just need to be an expert in your field; you need to be a well-rounded genius capable of talking about any subject, whether financial, political, or sports-related or something of nature. Consume knowledge like air and put your pursuit of learning above all else.

5. Focus on increasing your income.

Be thankful that you have several options to boost your revenue, like investing in high ROI businesses and side hustling.

My income was $3,000 per month, and then nine years later, it was $20,000 a month. Start following the money, and it will force you to control revenue and see opportunities.

"In today's economic environment, you cannot save your way to millionaire status, Grant Cardone, who went from being broke and in debt at the age of 21 to becoming a self-made millionaire by 30. "The first step is to focus on increasing your income in increments and repeating that.

6. Increase your streams of income.

After studying the wealthy for over five years, author Thomas Corley had discovered that 65 percent of self-made millionaires that he studied had three streams of income, 45 percent had four streams, and 29 percent had five or more streams.

This could include starting a side business, working part-time, making investments, and renting out everything from your home to your car to maybe household items.

7. Take advantage of America's lavishness.

You should use a broker or brokerage firm that charges very little per trade and not trade too frequently. I can advise you if you want to become a millionaire, you need to take all the help you can get.

Making sure your investment fees and tax bill are as low as possible will go a long way toward helping you achieve your goal."

If you have "a 401(k) or 403(b) through work, then any money you contribute to the account can grow tax-deferred, but allowing your money to compound more quickly.

Opening up a traditional or Roth IRA, because those plans keep Uncle Sam away from your money, either now or later."

"Of course, earning a high return on your nest egg is easier said and done, as many factors in creating that return are outside of your control.

However, all investors have control over two huge factors that can severely drag on long-term returns: investment costs and taxes.

If you want to become a millionaire, you need to focus on keeping both as low as possible.

The best way I know to become a millionaire is to put the power of compound interest on your side.

By giving your money more time to compound and keeping your rate of return as high as possible, you'll significantly increase your chances of reaching a six-seven-figure net worth.

There are so many people today with their sights set on big financial goals for the future. More specifically, many individuals are looking for the simplest ways to become a millionaire.

There is no end to the different types of approaches and suggestions out there that offer "theories" on becoming a millionaire.

While theories are grand, many aspiring millionaires need real action and steps to find the success they have been looking for. While it isn't always an easy road to reach this type of financial success, there are some tangible actions and steps that individuals can take to become a millionaire.

8. Automate your savings.

If you want to become a millionaire, then you need to get into the habit of saving by contributing to your 401(k), Roth, or Traditional IRA and contributing to an emergency fund account that's been placed in a money market fund. However, the way to make this work is by automating your savings. This will automatically withdraw a percentage of your salary and place it into your contributions without you ever seeing it. It's suggested that you put 10 percent toward investments and 5 percent toward savings. But it's all up to you to make the decisions.

How to Become a Millionaire Online This Year

1. Freelancing

Depending on your previous experience, personal interests, passions, connections, external factors in your life, level of motivation, some might be easier for you to start working on than others.

It's time to find out how to become a millionaire online. Keep in mind that the following business ideas are in no specific order.

If you're a complete newbie to online business, you might want to begin with freelancing.

That's how I began, too, with no experience, through focused work and improving my skills together with building new ones.

So you can start an agency and focus on finding clients and growing the business, while the freelancers will be doing what you once did yourself.

The Web is full of hard-working individuals who are already freelancing to make a living. But who'd like to be working for someone who provides security in their career that there will be clients every next month?

They don't need to be experts, just to be good enough freelancers for that same field.

If it goes well, you can hire 1-3 people and set aside time to train them. Once you understand how this works, you can leave the sites you're using and land your clients independently.

The truth is, billable hours won't make you rich. But the opportunities that come out of building a name for yourself and being known in that niche are tremendous.

The disadvantage of being a freelancer job is that it requires you to be behind a screen and get paid by the hour. And while it's not too ambitious to be charging $200-$400 per job in a year or two, it still won't be enough.

All of these are powerful life lessons that you'll be using from day to day up till after the day that you become a millionaire online.

Climbing the ladder can happen in 2 different ways:

- Keep raising your prices.
- Work more hours daily.

Then, you'll start with a fixed hourly rate, but it will be shallow depending on how fast you can work.

While you do it, however, you'll get an idea of how to communicate with clients, make sure you get paid on time, put more confidence in your work, negotiate, give them a great overall experience, ask for referrals, etc.

During that time, you will be building your portfolio.

As you're no one yet and the competition is enormous, you will be working on your own, creating projects, or doing work for free or for friends. Then, you'll need to build a website and showcase it. Now you're someone.

Then you need to take an online course or simply start reading about it and practicing it. With enough desire, you'll be ready to do it for clients within a few weeks. Ghostwriting or copywriting, Internet marketing, coding, web design, video editing, translating, etc. All these are and probably always will be in high demand.

If you're ready to start it on the side and then very soon leave your 9 to 5, then choose a skill that you're willing to build.

One way is to do your current jobs online and on your own, finding clients through platforms like Upwork, Freelancer, Fiverr, Guru, etc.

2. Find untapped niches.

You can also cultivate into existing and profitable niches and find sub-niches.

That means people's needs are unsatisfied. While further marketing research is necessary to see whether these people also have buyer's intention and are not just looking to read about it, it's still something you would want to consider.

Use free tools such as Google Keyword Planner and look for keywords that get searches every month, but there's no good content written.

If you're willing to be an Internet millionaire, you need to start doing extensive research to find untapped markets.

Entrepreneurship is for creative individuals that are willing to take risks, be the first to enter into a field, and test new products when they see that people might be interested in them.

Some of these companies that came up with more filters or ways to un-follow people fast, or automate comments and likes, are businesses for millions of dollars. The same goes for a new physical product like each new iPhone, for instance. That then creates the need for a new case or something. I hope you see my point.

For instance, when Instagram came out, many other software products offered services related to it. There are plenty of different ways to make money on Instagram, as well.

These are called unsaturated markets, and there's little to no competition there, but the demand is present.

Monetizing them once you find the one you're interested in and seeing the potential in it can happen in a few ways. As technology evolves, people's desires change, and creative people transform all fields online, it will always be possible to find untapped niches.

And you might be wondering how to become a millionaire online when the competition seems to be fierce in every possible niche. But that's not necessarily the case.

3. Have a Software world Service business.

If you think that the software world is for you, then start thinking of your million-dollar ideas for a tech product and begin validating it as soon as possible.

We live in the best possible times to learn how to become a millionaire online through a software product as investors are continually looking for new tech enthusiasts.

With a quick Google search, you'll find hundreds of articles that mention people's stories like that.

If you look at any list of millionaires across the globe, you'll notice that most of them are in the Tech part.

You're already using the products and services of software companies like these apps:

Google Apps

Zoom

Vimeo

Stripe

WPX Hosting

Calendar

Taboola

ConvertKit

Slack

Weekly

Duolingo

RescueTime

Github

Teachable

Squarespace

SEMrush

Grammarly

The main benefits of Software as a service include scalability, ease to use, integration with other systems, different pricing models that allow for subscription or a yearly plan that saves money, constant upgrades, and more.

While you will need to be a software engineer yourself or hire people for that matter, find investors for your startup and pitch them ably.

You can also validate your ideas online and get your first users onboard long before investing your time creating the actual product.

That's one of the slow and challenging career paths for aspiring millionaires, but thousands of examples of people got rich from one of their products.

In this list of digital products that you can choose from for the first time, you can build something online. I have mentioned having a software product.

4. Leverage Amazon Associates.

Once you figure out the best way for you after creating a few small niche sites and fill them with great content and links, and after you start earning your first money online as an Amazon associate, you can then scale up by creating 100 more sites like that, or entering new niches.

But that's what can help you earn hundreds and thousands of dollars every month.

Some products convert better than others do. There are strict rules to follow when being a part of the program.

And you're going to have sleepless nights creating long buyer's guides and writing reviews about boring products.

There are many tricks of the trade you'll need to learn to let an Amazon business turn you into an Internet entrepreneur.

Now, the point is to give potential buyers enough information about the product and let them find value in your posts, and stay on your site. They will then click on the links that will take them to the product page (this link will have your affiliate ID in its URL).

Choose a niche that you can quickly produce a lot of content around and make sure that products are directly related to it that people are already buying.

You can join the program today and start reading about how other affiliates are making money with it. The usual scenario requires a lot of work and strategizing in advance but can then turn into a passive income stream to create an Amazon Affiliate site.

But you can't go wrong with Amazon Associates simply because it's the most significant online retailer's affiliate program ever. No wonder its founder, Jeff Bezos, is the wealthiest person in the world right now.

While it's not a must to have your site for that but you can rely on other sites, such as newsletter and social media, those work best. There are different networks you can join, as well.

To be an affiliate means to earn a commission every time someone clicks on your unique link forwarding them to another platform.

While affiliate marketing itself is and will always have been a lucrative opportunity for those looking to earn cash online, one of the networks, in particular, is sure to give you the results if you get the hang of it.

5. Become a social media influencer.

Once you have the attention, you can then monetize it; that wasn't an option ten years ago. But it's another proof that we're now living in the era of opportunities because many other smart and hard-working people became millionaires online themselves and to do it by following this path.

These people often don't even think of turning this into a business, but can soon end up being self-made millionaires, thanks to their travel vlog, beauty tutorials, or Instagram feed with quotes or gym pictures.

But before you even realize that, you'll already be a brand, and sponsors will be emailing you every day.

Once you have the attention, you can then start monetizing it. That's because they appealed to a specific audience who subscribed to their channel or started following their profile and are engaged with their content.

What might seem unfair is that teenagers on Instagram, crazy kids, or bored adults on YouTube, and people with no necessary skills on other platforms became millionaires overnight.

This might sound like a sweet option for becoming a millionaire online, but it's not something that everyone can do.

6. Investing to become a millionaire.

Another way to become a millionaire online is to start investing.

Let's say, for example, if you want to understand how crypto-currencies work but have never read a single article about it, you'll need to invest at least 100 hours to be a beginner and feel comfortable making financial decisions in a fast-changing market.

This can be a fun game for the risk-takers and strategists that are out there. But it can be a nightmare for those who aren't okay with uncertainty and who won't sleep peacefully with so many numbers in their head.

From trading crypto-currencies, starting side hustles, investing in the stock market, and flipping websites or buying existing businesses.

Don't start big, even though. There are many things that you can do with your first $1000, for instance.

7. Make money from home by selling your knowledge.

If you're wondering where to sell your online courses, I'd recommend Teachable. It's super easy for anyone new to create a path from scratch and start getting students on board and earning money.

How can you get some of that money by providing value in return? Here's how to become a millionaire online in the educational sector:

- Create an online course and sell it on Teachable (people make millions from systems on these platforms).
- Teach English online through your website.
- Create an authoritative blog with articles on the topics that you know more about and build traffic. Then, write an eBook and sell it;
- Build a membership site and share premium content and other types of products with members.
- Start consulting in your area of expertise.

- Write guides for beginners and sell them on Amazon KDP.

Digital education is becoming normal right now. As Reuters shared, the e-learning industry is booming and is expected to reach $275 billion by 2022.

8. Get into E-Commerce.

So that's another way how you become a millionaire online. Easier said and done, though. Before you go and do your research on the list, you liked the most, here's more.

With drop shipping, you can buy products and get them delivered to a client.

While there's a lot of responsibility that goes with the shipment, the quality of such products, and your reputation, it often turns into a business for millions of dollars simply because the model is tested and it works.

But with technological advancement, you don't even need to see or touch that product to make a sale.

E-commerce will never die.

You'll always be selling. But the original idea is to make people buy actual physical products.

Whether it's ad space onto your site, brand mentions on social media, a digital product, a video course, an hour of your time to write something, or your skills to help somebody grow their business.

In the online world, anything that involves selling.

How and to whom might be different for everyone, but the basic principles behind this business model are still the same.

You should know how to promote a product and that you need to know what the customer wants, so you know that you can use their language when making an offer. One of the oldest ways that we use to make money is by selling stuff.

9. Bonus Ways to Become an Internet Millionaire

Work for a millionaire to create multiple income streams. Financial expert, entrepreneur, and one of my favorite people to follow online is Pat Flynn, who understood this a long time ago.

Thanks to his detailed monthly income reports, we're able to see exactly where that money is coming from. And it's not from one place at all.

That's why he made more than two million dollars last year.

But you can easily combine that with creating guides for beginners who want to do what you're doing and enter the e-learning market as well.

The more things you're offering and the more places that you appear on, the bigger the success you'll see.

Any platform that you rely on can go bankrupt at any time. Any niche can be replaced with another one. Your freelance business might not make enough.

For that to happen, you'll need to be making money online in more than one way.

To not just be a millionaire but also live like one, you'll need to have some free time to do things that you will enjoy, instead of always worrying about managing your money (that's a problem as well).

Then gather that experience, discipline, and mindset to create something on your own. What's best is to have a mentor. Many successful entrepreneurs suggested that something is to go and work for a millionaire for a few years and learn how their business and mind work.

Sometimes all we need to become a millionaire online is first to build our mindset necessary for that. But if ordinary people surround you, get distracted by all that's going on in your daily life more comfortable, and can't seem to be focused and stay consistent with your goals, and then you're going to have a problem.

14 things millionaires do differently from everyone else

1. They're frugal.

Spending above your means, overspending instead of saving for retirement, spending in anticipation of becoming wealthy makes you a slave to the paycheck, even with a stellar level of income; many of the millionaires stressed the freedom comes with spending below their means.

Frugality, a commitment to saving, spending less, and sticking to a budget is one of the wealth factors that help millionaires to build wealth, according to Sarah the Affluent Market Institute and also an author of "The Next Millionaire Next Door:

Enduring Strategies for Building Wealth," for which she surveyed more than 600 millionaires in America.

2. They keep their housing costs low.

Most of the millionaires she studied had never purchased a home that cost more than triple their annual income. The median home value for millionaires in her latest study was $850,000 (3.4 times their current revenue), with a median original buying price of $465,000.

A prime example of frugality is that millionaires typically live in a home and neighborhood that they can easily afford, saving a lot of their income.

If you make $350,000 and spend $350,000, "you are no better off at the end of the year.

While this savings rate might be slightly off because of things like not counting taxes as spending, the main takeaway is that millionaires "save a large portion of their income."

Marco, who ran the personal-finance blog ESI Money and retired at 52 with a $3 million net worth, has interviewed 100 millionaires over the past few years and found that the median millionaire spent

$90,000 a year while earning $250,000 in income, a 64% savings rate, saving it allows for investment.

Being frugal and living in an affordable home enables millionaires to save.

They will recognize that income isn't enough; they have to keep what they're making.

3. They have a budget.

A budget is great for the early phases of a financial plan, but if you can grow your income and develop self-discipline, and not overspend, it's not essential to your success later on.

While it's not expected, the reason why millionaires don't need a budget makes sense — they make a lot and have self-control. In other words, they make a ton, and spend only a portion of it, and have plenty left over. Who needs a budget?

But millionaires can be frugal and save without budgeting. Many of the millionaires that Marco spoke with said they didn't have a budget.

The average millionaires have made a habit of budgeting every month.

They know what's coming in and what's taken from their bank accounts. Budgeting is the key to winning with money. It's telling each dollar where to go at the beginning of the month instead of wondering where it all went.

Like you would build a house by starting with the foundation, it's the same way you build wealth by starting with the budgeting basics. And then you keep following them. When you're making a lot of money, you don't stop managing it.

Your budget is your plan. And you can't build a million-dollar net worth without a plan. Success isn't an accident. You are in charge of your wealth-building.

4. They take on a side hustles

Millionaires develop multiple streams of income, enabling them to grow their net worth exponentially.

Those who can create multiple opportunities to generate revenue, who can translate their hobbies into income, produce activities, and become millionaires next door in the future.

Many millionaires take on side hustles; it's an excellent way to explore options while remaining employed full time.

5. They invest in real estate.

Millionaires built wealth by investing in real estate, Dana Bull, a real-estate investor; the financial advantages of investing in real estate are plentiful: a positive cash flow, appreciation in housing values, leverage, and tax advantages.

Investing in real estate seems like a natural result once the basics are covered, and excess cash is generated.

6. They invest in low-cost index funds.

Experts agree that investing in index funds is a winning strategy when playing the stock market for two reasons: They're broadly diversified, eliminate the risk of picking individuals stocks, and they're low cost. Even Warren Buffett champions the strategy.

With the high returns and low costs of stock index funds, many millionaires also tend to use the same simple investing strategy: investing in low-cost index funds.

They put more energy into personal-growth activities.

Change Your Habits, Change Your Life, Marco, spent five years researching the daily habits of 177 self-made millionaires and found out that they devoted at least 30 minutes every day each to exercising and reading. Millionaires tend to read three types of books, and he said: biographies of successful people, self-help or personal development, and history.

Successful individuals are keenly aware of how they spend their resources, including their emotional and cognitive resources.

Millionaires also spend more time focusing on personal growth. They spend roughly 6 hours a week reading for pleasure and nearly 7 hours a week exercising. In comparison, the average American spends two hours and 2 1/2 hours on those activities, according to Marco's research. They spend more time studying and planning for investments.

Their literacy in financial matters defines that they are more tolerant of taking investment-related risks. Future outlook and financial knowledge typically relate to more significant financial trouble, so they spend time managing and researching investments in decision-making.

That's nearly two hours more than under-accumulators of wealth, defined that as those with a net worth less than one-half of their expected net worth based on age and earnings, who spend 8.7 hours a month doing so.

Millionaires preferred to invest in strategies that might be fueled by their research. Millionaire investors spend more time, an average of 10.5 hours a month, planning for investments.

7. They sleep less and work more.

Getting up at five in the morning to tackle the top three things you want to accomplish for the day allows you to regain control of your life. It gives you a sense of confidence that you'll, indeed, direct your life.

That might be because many wake up at least three hours before their workday begins — a strategy to deal with inevitable daily disruptions.

But millionaires make a few sacrifices to make the most of their time.

They sleep nearly eight hours less a week and work six hours more a week than the average American.

8. They think more.

They asked questions such as what can I do to earn more money? Does my job make me happy? Am I exercising enough? And what other charities can I get involved in?

"Thinking is the key to their success," They spent time every day brainstorming with themselves about numerous things.

The research found that self-made millionaires are thinkers. The rich tend to think in isolation in the mornings and for at least 15 minutes every day or more.

9. They ask for feedback.

It allows millionaires to change course and experiment with a new career or business. "Feedback provides you with the information you will need to succeed in any venture."

The fear of criticism is the reason we do not seek feedback from others.

But feedback is vital to learning what is working and what isn't working.

Feedback helps you to understand if you are on the right track. Feedback criticism, good or bad, is a crucial element for learning and growth. Millionaires seek feedback to help improve themselves and their businesses.

10. They don't follow the crowd.

You need to separate yourself from the weeds, create your weeds, and then get others to join them. Instead, successful people make their new weed.

We so desire to blend in, to acclimate to society, to be a part of the weed, that we will do almost anything to avoid standing out in a crowd.

Failure to separate yourself from the weeds is why most people never achieve success. Millionaires don’t follow the crowd.

11. They're resilient, and they persevere.

Millionaires and other economically successful Americans or others around the world who pursue self-employment decide to climb the corporate ladder or strive to create a financially independent lifestyle early do so by perpetually pushing on.

To build wealth, build one's own business, ignore critics and media and surrounding neighbors, you must have the resolve to keep pursuing your goals past rejection and pain; self-made millionaires use the resilience and perseverance characteristics of early retirees and entrepreneurs — to build wealth.

12. They prioritize four relationships.

Finding a mentor puts you on the fast track to wealth accumulation and the importance of having a particular mentor.

Everyday Millionaires: How Ordinary People Built Extraordinary Wealth — and How You Can Too.

Studies show 10,000 American millionaires — defined as those with a net worth of at least $1 million for seven months and found they achieved their seven-figure status with four key relationships: a coach, a mentor, a cheerleader, and a friend.

But one more thing, millionaires can't build wealth without the help of others.

13. They practice consistency.

Millionaires have known from experience that wealth-building is a long-term frame, and they have seen that sticking to the plan over decades leads to millions at retirement.

You can also take responsibility, you can be intentional, you can set goals, and you can work hard.

If you don't do these things repeatedly year after year, decade after decade, you'll never get the results you need.

According to Hogan, millions take personal responsibility, practice intentionality, are all goal-oriented and work hard.

While those are qualities of many people, millionaires recognize that these traits can't work together without consistency regardless of their net worth.

14. They're more conscientious.

Similarly, Jude Miller Burke studied 200 self-made millionaires for three years and found that they tended to be conscientious and displayed the trait at a higher level than less successful people.

Many of the behavioral components that impact net worth, regardless of how old we are or our income levels, including frugality, planning, and responsibilities, tie into his/her personality characteristic and help us to understand why it is so critical in the creation and maintenance of wealth over time.

Most millionaires' traits and habits tie into conscientiousness, which has a strong correlation to net worth.

ESERVE NOTE
6482A

Millionaire mindset success habits

11. Success Habits of Millionaire Mind-Sets

1. Millionaires exercise

You know you need just to do it! But psychology today's study has shown that being physically active positively influenced 15-year income. The study's physically active men earned between 14 and 17 percent more than their less active twins. Not every wealthy person does—we all know the fat cat stereotype.

2. Millionaires have a daily must-do list

Need help making the most of your must-to-do list? Before you go to bed, try writing down between three and six (no more) of the most important things you need to do tomorrow. Prioritize them, start with the number one item listed, and don't stop until it's complete.

Eighty percent of wealthy people said they kept their to-do lists, compared to 19 percent of those in poverty—two-thirds of rich listers complete 70 percent or more of their daily tasks.

3. Millionaires don't watch TV

We're not saying that you have to cancel your Netflix subscription or stop watching your television all to complete, but if you watch on the regular and you've ever claimed you don't have enough time to do something, well, you have your answer.

Only 23 percent of millionaires watch more than an hour of TV a day, compared with 77 percent of everybody else. That leaves time for wealthy folks to do other things that broaden their financial horizons.

This action item (or non-action item) has more to it than "Judge Judy" reruns being hazardous to your mental health. It's about the productive use of your time.

4. Millionaires read the financial times

The Financial Times may not be for everybody, but reading a global business publication-especially one that might challenge you to learn new things about business and finance, which is a good habit.

The Wall Street Journal and The Economist are others to consider.

But it appears that some folks are counting the wrong numbers.

The piece also cites FT's stats, which estimate an average subscriber income at $250,000—while 13 percent of readers are millionaires.

Go ahead, and make fun of those sissies, salmon-colored newsprint pages; the FT crowd is laughing all the way to the bank.

5. Millionaires are healthy eaters.

If you want to change your eating habits, skip fad diets. Instead, start treating your food like the fuel it is. Eat just enough of the right foods to power through your workday or your workout. Save and stay away from junk meals and snacks. Leave them for special occasions when you can enjoy them guilt-free.

This problem is undoubtedly complex: less-affluent consumers may have a more challenging time accessing healthier foods due to income and geography, but successful people are also more focused on their diet and overall health and more willing to seek out (and spend more on) healthy foods.

It's hard to get your money-making brain into high gear if you feed it on Twinkies and Cheetos all day long.

And the sad news is that the diets of low-income people are getting worse, while those of high-income people are improving, according to a study in the Journal of the American Medical Association, Internal Medicine.

6. Millionaires prioritize self-improvement

Want to make it work for you?

Choose one thing that you want to do more of exercise, learning a new skill, creating, and blocking out time each day or each week to work on it.

Treat your appointment like any other and commit to showing up.

New York Times bestselling author Brendon Burchard—who hangs out with Bill Gates and Richard Branson—consistently blocks out time to create. He calls it a habit of the super successful.

It's one thing to say you want to get better at something; it's another thing to make it a priority and do it.

7. Millionaires rise early

If you love the snooze button, this one is tricky, I know. Start small by waking up five minutes earlier than you usually do. If you're serious about becoming an early riser, check out Hal Elrod's The Miracle Morning. It's a program that helps you gradually incorporate things that you love to do into the first minutes or hour of your day, so, eventually, you can't wait to leap out of bed instead of hiding from the world under the covers.

The majority of these individuals are up at five-thirty or six a.m., slaving away while the rest of us are still eating pancakes. The early bird gets more than the worm; it seems.

8. Millionaires never stop learning

Every day, download a business or self-improvement podcast for your next 30-minute drive or treadmill session. Alternatively, check out one of these essential personal finance books.

Whatever the forum is, wealthy folks are absorbing more knowledge. Research shows that 63 percent of the wealthy listen to audiobooks during a commute to work.

Audiobooks, Podcasts, Real books, TED Talks on YouTube

Not all readers are leaders, but all leaders are readers. One of the reasons why millionaires become millionaires is because of their constant desire to learn. To them, leadership books and biographies are much more important than the latest reality show or who got kicked off the island. When they have free time, they use it very wisely—by reading.

9. Millionaires Give.

And that's actually why they continue building their wealth. They realize that they can't take it with them if or when they should die. Instead of spending it all on the latest toys, they choose to leave a legacy for the people who mean the most to them.

Whether it's tithing at church, donating to a charity, or just giving to friends and family, these people have generous spirits. They realized that the most important thing you can do with wealth is to help others.

Sure, some rich people can be selfish jerks just like anyone else. But the everyday millionaires that live down the street, the ones you don't even realize that are wealthy, are some of the most giving people you'll ever meet. I know because I've met a lot of them. They work hard, save, and respect the ability of others to do just the same.

10. Millionaires stay away from debt.

Debt is the biggest obstacle to building wealth. I tell everyone. They need to avoid it; it's like a plague. Your dreams are too important!

Car payments, student loans, same-as-cash financing plans just aren't part of their vocabulary. That's why they win with money. They don't owe anything to the bank, so every dollar they earn stays with them to spend, save, and give!

One of the biggest myths out there is that the average millionaires see "debt as a tool." Not true. If they want something they can't afford, they save and pay cash for it later.

11. Millionaires understand delayed gratification.

Every day, millionaires spend most of their lives, sacrificing temporary pleasures for long-term success.

They have no problem buying an older used car, living in a modest neighborhood, and wearing inexpensive clothes. They don't seem to care about keeping up with the Joneses.

Preference of millionaire men and women

This isn't the first survey to look at what types of people are preferable to date. A study from August 2013 found out that people who save a lot of money are more desirable than those who spend a lot of money. And a survey from July 2012 found out that dating is easier for "hot women.

The survey also found that rich women would be more careful with their wealth if they entered into a marriage than rich men. Eighty-two percent of the female respondents said they would insist on a prenuptial agreement, while only 17.4 percent of the male respondents would do the same.

The female millionaires surveyed indicated that they are not looking to take care of anybody and prefer a financially stable partner.

We were shocked to learn that the vast majority of our male millionaire members sought non-millionaires. It seems that financially independent men want to share their wealth with those that are less fortunate. With women, the story is much different.

Darren Shuster, a representative for MillionaireMatch.com, said in a press release that rich men don't want to date rich women because they want a partner they can care for.

The site surveyed a random sample of nearly 15,000 members to discern what type of women millionaires prefer to date.

The results revealed that the vast majority of millionaire men, 79.6 percent, seek out non-millionaire women, while 84.5 percent of the female millionaires would prefer to date another millionaire.

According to a new survey by MillionaireMatch.com, the dating site for millionaires, rich men do have very different dating preferences than their female counterparts.

This would not be the first time MillionaireMatch.com has looked at the dating preferences of its users. I mean, Back in September, the site surveyed its members and found out that a majority of millionaire men, 79.6 percent, seek out non-millionaire women, while 84.5 percent of the female millionaires would prefer to date another millionaire like themselves.

It was a different story for women on the site.

A whopping 67.9 percent of divorced female millionaires said: "no thanks" to marrying again or would even wait at least ten years or more before tying the knot.

A mere 32.1 percent of female millionaires said that they were willing to consider remarrying in the next five years or less.

MillionaireMatch.com, the dating site for the rich, actually surveyed 5,000 divorced millionaire members and found 83.4 percent of wealthy men would consider remarrying in the next five years, while only 5.2 percent never said ever again.

But 11 percent said they would consider tying the knot after five years.

For example, Kanye West and Jamie Foxx may have recorded "Gold Digger" from a guy's perspective. Still, a new survey of millionaires looking for love suggests that it's millionaire women, not millionaire men, who are most apprehensive about remarrying.

Traveling Millionaire: North Shore, Oahu, Hawaii

Lodging

Airbnb: $120 per night, $150 cleaning fee, $50 service fee.

We stayed three nights for $560, and the total nightly rate is $186. We stayed at the Magnolia Loft, and it was the place to die for! Looking at such cute and updated expectations and absolutely to perfection.

Our hosts were so generous and kind, and we would 100% recommend anyone to stay here.

We chose moderately priced accommodation, but there are even less expensive places to stay in the same area. Please note that prices vary depending on the season.

Hotel option: The cheapest rooms are available at Turtle Bay. (The only hotel in the area) was $307 per night, which would have been $921 for our three nights before paying for on-site parking, which is ($15 per night) or any resort fees ($48.17 per night). With all these fees, we would have been in for $1,107.51 for three nights! Well, we stayed three nights right down the way (literally only a 1-minute drive) for $547 less. I will take that any day!

Food

Restaurants in this area are pricey, and while the food is good, this area is not known as being a foodie place. You should consider that when deciding where you would want to eat while staying on the North Shore.

Also, the whole island is known for its Acai bowls. These were somewhat of an obsession for us actually while we were in Hawaii. We had them every single day for breakfast or an early lunch.

Two great options on the North Shore are the Haleiwa Bowls and the Sunrise Shack. While not an inexpensive breakfast (bowls are $8 and up), they are so refreshing and, of course, worth it.

The way to go on the North Shore is food trucks.

There are many different types of food trucks parked around where you can even sample some of the island's best inexpensive food.

We love the food truck experience because you can test a bunch of different kinds of food! If you have done any research about being on the North Shore, you will have heard someone mention Garlic Shrimp.

While it seems necessary, it is incredibly delicious! Large shrimp are served with a side dish of white rice.

Below is a centrally located food truck round-up, where we tried many different types of food and loved it all!

Tip from our friends who live on Oahu: before driving up to the North Shore, you can buy any snacks, alcohol, or groceries in Honolulu as the grocery store prices on the North Shore (Foodland Pūpūkea) are much higher during the tourism season.

Drinks

We opted to buy ourselves beverages from the grocery store and sip them at Shark's Cove at sunset instead of paying for expensive drinks at a bar both nights.

As I have mentioned earlier, the best plan of action to save money is to buy your alcoholic beverages in Honolulu and bring them with you to the North Shore.

Rental Car

Rental Car Company: Looking at the cars on the rental car sites, it was at least $90 per day to go through these companies actually to rent a Jeep.

With our three day rental, we saved $90 here!

Turo: we knew that we wanted to rent a Jeep as we drove around the island and decided to check Turo car Rental Company.

We had never rented from them before, but since they are the "Airbnb" of car rentals, we decided to give it a try! We paid $60 per day for a super cool soft-top Jeep to take the top down when we wanted to—cue Treslyn's sunburn.

Overall, Turo was super easy and helped to save us money. Use our Turo link to save $25 on your first rental!

FREE Entertainment

Overall, we enjoyed all that the North Shore has to offer and avoid overspending! The biggest tips would be to rent an Airbnb instead of staying at an expensive hotel, dining at the food trucks vs. overpriced restaurants, and using Turo car rental, to rent a car instead of a traditional rental car company.

This is the perfect beach spot for the day! Bring your lunch, some drinks, and sunscreen, and you are set for a day of fun in the sun.

Banzai pipeline: have you ever wondered where professional surfers would go to catch some serious waves? Well, this is it! We went to the Banzai pipeline two afternoons to watch surfers ride these gnarly waves. After watching all these giant waves roll in, you will have a completely different appreciation for the sport of surfing.

The Secrets of the Millionaire Mind

Think of ways that will support you in your happiness and success

Research has shown that when people work with a positive mindset, their performance on almost every level equal productivity, creativity, and engagement with others improves. Yet still, happiness is perhaps one of the most misunderstood drivers of performance.

Most people believe that success precedes happiness.

People who typically cultivate a positive mind-set perform better in the face of challenges.

I called it the "happiness advantage" every business, and a person's outcome shows improvement when the brain is positive.

Another common misconception is that our genetics, and our environment, are a combination of the two determines how happy we are.

The truth is, both factors have an impact. But an individual general sense of well-being is surprisingly malleable.

The habits you cultivate, how you interact with coworkers, and how you think about stress can increase your happiness and chances of success.

You are the one that is aware that your thoughts will lead to your feelings and then to actions. You have the choice to change the way you think.

You Can't Help Procrastinating?

Let's say, for instance, and you're avoiding a particular task because you find it boring or unpleasant, so you're going take steps how to get it out of the way quickly so that you can focus on the aspects of your job that you find more enjoyable or relaxing.

Analyze your procrastination problem quickly by assessing them. You will also find out why you have been procrastinating and how to overcome it.

Your life is not just about you. It's also about helping others.

Our lives are not just about living right to our mission, and the reason for being here on this earth at this time is to help others. It's about adding your piece of the puzzle to the world. Most people are so stuck in their egos that everything revolves around them and more of them. But if you want to be rich in the most real sense of the word, it can't only be about you. It has to include adding value to other people's lives.

If you envy the rich, you'll stay broke

Many of us can admit to stealing and hiding money to inflate our lifestyle, including money spent maintaining at least one extra-marital affair. We've all seen this kind of behavior before, if not with ourselves but with others. There are many high-profile politicians, lobbyists, athletes, and entertainers who had shown us the downside of overspending even when they earned more than some of us will ever make in our lifetime.

The point is to bless that which you want. Admire, blessing, and love the rich if you're going to be rich.

This goes for everything that you want in your life.

When you're tempted to envy the rich, just think about what they may be doing to live high and mighty.

The more you give, the more get

There's an old saying: stating that it is better to give than to receive. The interpretation of this is that giving is an act of kindness. There's another old saying: The more you give, the more you will get. So, the act of giving truly is an act of kindness, even if you know that you'll receive something back, and even if you don't know exactly what it is? I think so, especially if the act of giving has no strings attached – even if giving more means you'll get more, then it is truly an act of kindness.

To give, you will receive, and it's vice versa. There must be a receiver for every giver, and for every receiver, there must be a giver.

Our beliefs

Many of our thoughts and beliefs are formed outside of ourselves at home, in school, at church, on the radio/TV, or from books.

We're bombarded by the opinions of others, most of which we have taken on.

Being aware of this will help you to question some of what you do and believe.

The other component of change is to have an understanding.

Understanding where your way of thinking originates from will recognize that it has to come from outside you.

This is the key to all changes! When you are aware that your thoughts lead to feelings, your feelings lead to actions, and your steps lead to results, you can then begin to make changes.

The first element of change is awareness. You can't change something unless you know that it exists.

When thinking about making changes, one of the first questions to always ask yourself is, why do I need this?

Is Will getting this change anything about my situation?

No amount of money can make you happy, safe, or good enough. If you are not aware of the root of these feelings, you will keep creating them.

Motivation

The process of motivation is consists of three stages

1. A felt for need or drive
2. A spur in which needs have to be aroused
3. When our needs are satisfied, the satisfaction or accomplishments of goals are met.

Therefore, we can honestly say that motivation is a psychological phenomenon, which means that the individuals' needs and wants have to be tackled by framing an incentive plan.

If your basis for acquiring money or success comes from a non-supportive background such as fear, anger, or the need to 'prove' yourself, your money will neither bring you happiness nor motivate you.

Adding values to our life

Our Seventh Generation philosophy states that we consider the effects of our actions and decisions for seven generations into the future. Everything we do has consequences for something and someone else, and ultimately, we are all somehow connected.

The purpose of our lives is to add value to the people of this generation and those that follow.

Judging

When you look at someone's face, you'll see all the features of their face, eyes, nose, mouth, chin, hair, and so on.

All of these are neutral.

Then you might add blue eyes, big nose, tiny mouth, and pointed chin, beautiful or ugly, and you'll give it the qualities based on personal perceptions.

Without the judgments, there is no meaning to a thing just as it is. Nothing has meaning except for the sense that you give it.

What you focus on expands.

When you are focused on lack of money, opportunities, education, luck, and breaks, this will be what you get.

Change your focus to prosperity, infinite possibilities, doors opening, and miracles happening. This shift has the power to change your life and expand.

The power of money

If you're unhappy, afraid, feeling unworthy, or insecure, money is not going to change all of these. Money might even make things worse.

For example, if you're feeling unsure about money, then having more money may add to this as you ponder what to do with it, grow it, and keep it safe.

The money will only make you more of what you already are. In other words, money is the root of all evil.

The goal

Most people start things, but with the slightest amount of distraction, they get sidetracked from the goal; maybe it is a business, an exercise routine, or a dietary change.

If you want something, you have to keep your plan in sight. Keep your eye on the goal; keep moving toward your target or goal.

The invisible is the things that others cannot see, but your thoughts and beliefs... Most of us run on auto-pilot and pay little attention to our thoughts and ideas. Only when you do pay attention to these can you make changes.

If you want to change the fruits, you will first have to change the roots. If you're going to change the visible, you must first change the invisible.

Most when asked. The number one reason most people don’t get what they want is that they don’t know what they want.

Conclusion

There's 21 years old, who's been working for five years, and always scrambles to make ends meet at the end of the month, the 39-year-old who then realized that she is precisely modeled with her parent's financial behaviors and anyone who keeps pointing fingers at the government, their boss or the economy.

- Where and when our financial hard drive programs are shaped
- What's your money blueprint is and how it's imprinted with a few single sentences
- How to take inventory of your current mindset and financial status
- What can we do to break the patterns using affirmations?
- The kind of commitment does it takes to get rich and where to start

- Why can't you become a millionaire by thinking about a steady income first?
- How do you allocate your money each month in exact percentages?
- Why do future millionaires have to be a bit cocky to succeed

This book has a few "Wealth Files" that describe millionaires' habits and mindsets in detail.

Which makes a lot of sense once you catch on but is not something you'd think of yourself. I can relate to the predisposition part; we sometimes just adapt to what our parents do in every facet of life. It's natural, so if we need something different, we need to change our thought patterns.

So quit the complaints and start to objectively look at what you have to do, then take those necessary steps so that you can start learning from the right people.

I've done this before. I'd think of problems, I'd have once got rich, I have such friends that are only wanting for my money, or that being rich might make me a wrong person – this is nuts. First of all, it's not a problem for you, and I currently have, so don't waste time and energy trying to resolve it. Secondly, it's improbable to happen.

Having a positive attitude towards wealth and money is a prerequisite of attracting it. That doesn't mean that you should show off all the time, but you can't envy or mistrust current millionaires while you're hoping to become one yourself.

Thinking with such a scarcity mindset will almost block you from engaging with millionaires, learning from their material, and truly embracing what they have to teach you.

If you hate rich people, you will never get rich quickly.

Stop complaining, analyze where you're spending too much of your money, and adjust accordingly.

But the truth is, you're the one that is in the driver's seat and have been all along.

Realizing you're the one who's in control of all of your finances is the first step to making a change.

Instead of just sitting in the backseat, watching your money disappear, while blaming the government, your employer, or the economy, step up to your job as a bus driver. You will decide who gets off at which stop, no one else!

When you think of this metaphor, do you see yourself sitting in the very last row, just watching all of your precious dollar bills leave the bus, with someone else in the driver's seat? It's not uncommon for us to wonder at the end of the month, "Where did it all go?" and feeling like a victim because so many others have taken all of our actual money.

Let's paint a mental picture. At the beginning of the month, your paycheck has arrived.

Now imagine every dollar bill is a passenger on the bus, and over a month, that bus drives along, and everyone gets off at a different stop. Some dollars leave at the rent stop, and some leaves at the grocery stop, some get off at the dry cleaner's, and so on.

Realize you're the one that is in charge, to start taking control of your money. While it's entirely natural, replicating our parents' income habits won't work for most of us, we strive for more, after all – but what can you do to break old these thought patterns?

Not only is it widespread for sons of doctors to become doctors and daughters of lawyers to become lawyers, but also for us to just take the same approach to our careers overall that we've seen our parents take in our entire life.

If your dad has a regular job, you'll probably also get a regular job. If your parents own a business, you're more likely to start one at a young age, and as well.

If that sounds pretty much familiar, then you're in for a treat: Now, look at how you make your money.

Does it or maybe resemble almost precisely what your parents have done for years?

Your mum would then tell you a recipe for a cake and help you make it right.

But when you ask her why you are doing things in a certain way, her answer might be: “Well, that’s the way I’ve learned to do it from your grandma; it’s the way we’ve always made a chocolate cake.

Imagine your Mum makes an excellent chocolate cake (I hope she does!) and you wanted to bake one yourself. You’d probably turn to her for some advice and ask: “Hey Mum, how do I make that chocolate cake?

You will probably try to make money the same way your parents do.

Here are three lessons to get you to start changing your financial mindset:

1. You’ll naturally tend to replicate your parents’ income strategies.
2. If you want to control your finances, you’ll first have to realize that you’re the one at the wheel.
3. Don’t despise wealthy people.

As it turns out, some habits of the rich make or break whether you’ll become financially independent.

After riding an emotional and financial rollercoaster in the process of building, selling, and losing more than a dozen businesses, going from broke to millions and back, I started to analyze my relationship with money and my habits.

I first read T. Harv Eker's name in Hal Elrod's book, The Miracle Morning, because he was a mentor. Hal sometimes talks about living a "level ten life" where you'll be successful in all areas, not just one, and I have learned that from that book.

FAQ

How do millionaire think differently

Have you ever thought about the number of things that you have changed during your lifetime? You change your:

- Hair
- Address
- Job
- Clothing
- Spouse
- Friends
- Salary
- Attitude
- Behavior

But if you don't change your mindset, meaning that your mind or your dominant way of thinking, you will perpetuate the same experience repeatedly for the rest of your life because everything about you outwardly changed, but nothing inwardly about you has changed. There's nothing in the world that can rival a changed mind.

A new mindset will give you a new perspective on life. You will see things a different way by looking at your current circumstances. Whatever problem you are currently experiencing, know that the world matches us with opponents to make us stronger.

How do I get a million-dollar mindset

If you're the kind of person who likes to take the initiative and grow and do the things that you do every single day and knock off that to-do list, then get ready to hit it out of the park as an entrepreneur.

When making the transition to be working for yourself, it's entirely too easy to take advantage of the freedom it allows you to have.

You'll have to be accountable for every minute of your day, especially when it comes to initiating the tasks it takes to make you successful. Nobody is going to do the work for you. If you sit there and waste your time, your business will eventually wither on the vine and die.

How can I be like a millionaire

When you look like a million bucks and act like a million buck, you are at your millionaire mindset, regardless of the number showing up in your bank account, but before you worry about going to earn more, figure out where will you be spending the majority of your time and doing what to get that cash flow that you're yearning for.

What is it like to be a multimillionaire

From a witness' perspective, being a millionaire just allows you to have more freedom on a day to day basis.

They also have the same day to day issues as we all do with health, relationships and work, life balance. In a lot of cases, they work long hours and very hard.

Remember that the bigger the lifestyle, the more it costs to maintain it. If you, your friends, and your family have good health and are generally happy, then you are indeed a multi-millionaire. No matter how much money you have, you cannot buy health or happiness.

CPSIA information can be obtained
at www.ICGtesting.com
Printed in the USA
BVHW090424300421
606133BV00004B/384